DIS

BASIC

BELIEFS

SIX STUDIES FOR GROUPS
OR INDIVIDUALS
WITH NOTES FOR LEADERS

KEITH HUNT

ZondervanPublishingHouse
Grand Rapids, Michigan
A Division of HarperCollins*Publishers*

Requests for information should be addressed to:
Zondervan Publishing House
Grand Rapids, MI 49530

ISBN 0-310-54701-6

Edited by Jack Kuhatschek
Cover design by Tammy Grabrian Johnson
Cover illustration by Britt Taylor Collins
Interior design by Ann Cherryman

Printed in the United States of America

96 97 98 99 00 / ❖ DP / 12 11 10 9 8 7 6 5

Contents

The Discipleship Series

Welcome to The Discipleship Series, a unique new program designed with one purpose in mind—to make you a stronger, more effective disciple of Jesus Christ.

Whether you are a new Christian, a newly committed Christian, or someone who simply wants a deeper walk with God, The Discipleship Series can help you reach your goal of spiritual maturity.

You'll be learning from people who are known for their wisdom and godly example. The authors of this series are not armchair theologians, but seasoned veterans who have been disciples and disciplemakers for many years. Step by step they will guide you through the essentials of what it means to follow Christ and to become more like him.

The Discipleship Series is designed to be flexible. You can use the guides in any order that is best for you or your group. They are ideal for Sunday-school classes, small groups, one-on-one relationships, or as materials for your quiet times.

Because each guide contains only six studies, you can easily explore more than one facet of discipleship. In a Sunday-school class, any two guides can be combined for a quarter (twelve weeks), or the entire series can be covered in a year.

Each study deliberately focuses on a limited number of passages, usually only one or two. That allows you to see each passage in its context, avoiding the temptation of prooftexting and the frustration of "Bible hopscotch" (jumping from verse to verse). If you would like to look up additional passages, a Bible concordance will give the most help.

The Discipleship Series helps you *discover* what the Bible says rather than simply *telling* you the answers. The questions encourage you to think and to explore options rather than merely to fill in the blanks with one-word answers.

Leader's notes are provided in the back of each guide. They show how to lead a group discussion, provide additional information on questions, and suggest ways to deal with problems that may come up in the discussion. With such helps, someone with little or no experience can lead an effective study.

Suggestions for Individual Study

1. Begin each study with prayer. Ask God to help you understand the passage and to apply it to your life.

2. A good modern translation, such as the *New International Version*, the *New American Standard Bible*, or the *New Revised Standard Version*, will give you the most help. Questions in this guide, however, are based on the *New International Version*.

3. Read and reread the passage(s). You must know what the passage says before you can understand what it means and how it applies to you.

4. Write your answers in the space provided in the study guide. This will help you to clearly express your understanding of the passage.

5. Keep a Bible dictionary handy. Use it to look up any unfamiliar words, names, or places.

Suggestions for Group Study

1. Come to the study prepared. Careful preparation will greatly enrich your time in group discussion.

2. Be willing to join in the discussion. The leader of the group will not be lecturing but will encourage people to discuss what they have learned in the passage. Plan to share what God has taught you in your individual study.

3. Stick to the passage being studied. Base your answers on the verses being discussed rather than on outside authorities such as commentaries or your favorite author or speaker.

4. Try to be sensitive to the other members of the group. Listen attentively when they speak, and be affirming whenever you can. This will encourage more hesitant members of the group to participate.

5. Be careful not to dominate the discussion. By all means participate! But allow others to have equal time.

6. If you are the discussion leader, you will find additional suggestions and helpful ideas in the leader's notes at the back of the guide.

Introducing Basic Beliefs

A friend of mine once decided he could no longer believe in Jesus. For months he had struggled with doubts about his faith: "Is the Bible really true, or is it merely a collection of myths and wishful thinking?" "Is Jesus really God's Son, or was he deified by sincere but misguided followers?" Although my friend *wanted* to believe, he also wanted to be intellectually honest.

Alone one evening, he offered a final desperate prayer: "Lord, if you do exist, please help me. My doubts are overwhelming me!" But the silence that followed seemed to smother the last flickers of his faith.

The next day he began to realize the enormity of his decision. He had planned on attending seminary after graduation. Now what would he do with his life? He had tried to follow biblical teachings about morality. Now the very words *right* and *wrong* seemed meaningless. He had placed all his future hopes and dreams on Jesus Christ. Now there was no future—at least none that compared to what Christ offered! Having rejected the foundation of his life, my friend watched in horror as the entire superstructure of his life collapsed around him.

Standing amid the "rubble," he remembered Peter's response to Jesus when asked if he and the other disciples wanted to desert him: "Lord, to whom shall we go? You have the words of eternal life" (John 6:68). With quiet resolve, my friend made Peter's words his own and recommitted his life to Christ. He didn't ignore or suppress his doubts, but decided to search harder for answers. (His doubts were eventually resolved.)

Certain basic beliefs are central to our faith as Christians. These beliefs are not abstract theological concepts that have little to do with reality. They provide a foundation and framework for our daily lives—how we think, what we value, why we plan and work and hope. These beliefs give meaning and purpose to our lives in a way that nothing else can.

This guide looks at basic beliefs. Any attempt to compress the richness and variety of the Christian faith into six brief studies may seem presumptuous. Yet the basic concepts of Christianity are not difficult. Within these studies you will be able to investigate the teachings that form the backbone of the Christian faith.

These are big themes that will not be exhausted by a few hours study. Don't let the size of the project discourage you. Remember the wise man who told a friend how to eat an elephant—one bite at a time!

Keith Hunt

Isaiah 40:9–31

The Greatness of God

A recent issue of a news magazine included an article on the boating craze in America. Bill, an unmarried thirtyish patent lawyer, was quoted as saying: "Why did I buy a power-boat instead of a sailboat? I don't want to rely on God to get me home!"

Although his remark was intended as a joke, it probably reveals some of his true feelings about God. People who claim to believe in God are often unwilling to trust him for the simplest areas of their lives—putting food on the table, providing them a place to live, or even getting them safely back to dry land. They pay lip service to God, but in practice they are little different than atheists.

In this study the prophet Isaiah urges us to cast away our puny concepts of God and to rediscover his greatness.

1. What, in your opinion, is Bill's real view of God?

2. Read Isaiah 40:9–31. What is the message that Isaiah instructs the messenger to announce (vv. 9–10)?

3. What qualities of God does Isaiah focus on in each of the following verses?

❑ verse 11:

❑ verse 12:

❑ verses 13–14:

❑ verses 15–17:

4. How does the description of God in verses 11–17 emphasize that he is beyond comparison (v. 18)?

5. Given the greatness of God, why is it foolish to worship idols (vv. 18–20)?

What "idols" are we tempted to worship today?

6. According to Isaiah, what should we have known and heard about God since the beginning of time (vv. 21–24)?

7. We understand size or power best when comparisons are used. What comparisons does Isaiah use to establish the wisdom and power of God (vv. 25–26)?

8. Why do you think God needs to remind us initially in verse 18 and again in verse 25 that no person (or thing) compares to him?

9. The complaint that "my way is hidden from the LORD" (v. 27) might reflect feelings that either (a) God is unable to discover my well-hidden way, or (b) he is so great and my way is so insignificant that he isn't interested in me. In the context, which option seems to be correct?

10. Having considered the extent of God's power and might, does Israel's complaint make sense—or not? Explain.

11. Note the repetition of "weary" (vv. 28–31). To whom is it applied?

If you are weary, what hope is given in these verses?

12. What three pictures of motion requiring energy are presented (v. 31)?

What are the energy demands of each type of motion?

13. To whom are the promises of renewed strength given (v. 31)?

How does Isaiah's description of God encourage you to "hope in the LORD?"

Supplemental Verses:
❑ God as holy and pure: Leviticus 19:2; 20:26
❑ God as Creator: Genesis 1–2; John 1:3; Colossians 1:16
❑ God as Father: Isaiah 63:16; Matthew 6:9
❑ God as Trinity: John 15:26; 16:7
❑ God as love: 2 Chronicles 7:3; 1 John 4:8

Memory Verse

Those who hope in the LORD *will renew their strength. They will soar on wings like eagles; they will run and not grow weary, they will walk and not be faint.*

Isaiah 40:31

Between Studies

Look up the supplemental verses, perhaps one a day. Think about the characteristics of God being considered and how they relate to the study in Isaiah 40.

Apply the promise of renewed strength from Isaiah 40:31 to a problem you face this week.

Psalm 19

Revelation

Earth's crammed with heaven,
And every common bush afire with God.
Elizabeth Barrett Browning

In the early days of space flight a Russian cosmonaut reported that he had been to the edge of space but had not seen God. Although his statement was ridiculed by most people, it did raise an interesting question: How can we relate to a God who is invisible—who is beyond the range of sight and sound and touch and taste and smell? How can finite people like us know One who is infinite?

The answer, of course, is that we cannot. It is impossible to know God or anything about him—unless he chooses to make himself known. Fortunately, he has made that choice.

God's passion to communicate caused him to write not one but two great books. The first was described by Galileo when he wrote: "Philosophy is written in this grand book—I mean the universe—which stands continually open to our gaze." The second book is Holy Scripture, in which God declares not only his glory but also how we may come to know him personally.

Psalm 19 describes how God speaks to us through both types of revelation: his world and his Word.

1. Have you ever tried to explain to a child something he or she didn't understand? How successful (or unsuccessful) were you? Why?

How does your experience compare to God's attempt to communicate with us?

2. Read Psalm 19. What titles would you give to the three major divisions of the psalm?

❑ verses 1–6:

❑ verses 7–11:

❑ verses 12–14:

3. What are some of the things the natural world reveals to us about God (vv. 1–6)?

4. What have you learned about God from observing the natural world?

5. What additional titles are used to describe the "law of the LORD" (vv. 7–11)?

6. What are some of the benefits we receive from God's written revelation (vv. 7–11)?

How do each of these benefits relate to the words the psalmist uses to describe God's Word ("perfect," "trustworthy," and so on)?

7. To what are the ordinances of the Lord compared (vv. 10–11)?

For our culture today, what other comparisons might you use?

8. How would you define the two kinds of sins David describes (vv. 12–13)?

9. Which kind of sins are worst: those we are unaware of or those we do deliberately? Explain.

How can God help us with both kinds of sins (vv. 12–14)?

10. How do the three titles of God (v. 14) help us to understand who he is and how we should relate to him?

11. Think back over the entire psalm. How does it motivate you to respond to God's glory in nature and in Scripture?

Supplemental Verses
❑ Responding to God's Word: 1 Thessalonians 2:13
❑ The benefits of Scripture: 2 Timothy 3:16
❑ The Spirit's role in Scripture: 2 Peter 1:20–21

Memory Verse
The heavens declare the glory of God; the skies proclaim the work of his hands.

Psalm 19:1

21

Between Studies

Take time this week to meditate on the natural world and on Scripture. One way to do this is a "retreat of silence." Go to a quiet and beautiful spot near your home where you can be alone with God for an hour or two.

Spend some of your time reflecting on God's glory in the beauty around you. What do you learn about him? What insights do you gain?

Spend the remainder of your time reading and meditating on one of the psalms. How is its wisdom like fine gold? How are its words as sweet as honey?

Genesis 1:24–31
Romans 3:9–20

Human Nature

In the book Dr. Jekyll and Mr. Hyde, *author Robert Lewis Stevenson explores the two sides of human nature. Dr. Jekyll represents what is good in humanity. He is a physician dedicated to healing the sick and caring for those who suffer. But his alter ego, Mr. Hyde, is a hideous creature, who stalks the streets of London looking for those he can attack and kill.*

Although Dr. Jekyll and Mr. Hyde looked different, had different names, and appeared at different times, they were, in fact, two struggling sides of one person. In that respect, Stevenson's portrait was biblical. The Bible will not allow us to have an extreme view of human nature that views it as entirely good or bad. As we will see in Genesis and Romans, we are both wonderfully made and deeply fallen.

---

1. How would you explain the fact that one child can grow up to be a Hitler and another a Mother Theresa?

Wonderfully Made

2. Read Genesis 1:24–31. What does God create on the sixth day?

3. Each day of creation begins with the words, "And God said . . ." (see vv. 3, 6, 9, 14, 20, 24). How is this phrase and what *normally* follows different from the words at the beginning of verse 26?

4. How is man similar to the animals created in verses 24–25?

How is he different?

5. In what specific ways do the man and woman have a dignity that transcends the beasts?

How does this reflect on the responsibility we have in caring for the world?

6. Why do you think the image of God requires more than a male alone (v. 27)?

7. How does God's evaluation of his work at the end of the earlier days of creation compare with his statement at the end of day six (v. 31)?

How should his evaluation affect your sense of worth?

Deeply Fallen

8. Read Romans 3:9–20. Note that we are now in the midst of a major section that deals with *sin* (Romans 1–3). How would you describe humans if this text were the whole story?

9. Why is it impossible to be "declared righteous" in God's sight by observing the law?

10. How does the description of humanity in Genesis contrast with that in Romans?

How is it possible for both to be true?

11. Because of Jesus Christ, God accepts us just as we are. Yet because we are fallen, God will not be satisfied until we are fully restored to his image. How can we live with this tension without becoming either complacent or overly self-critical?

Supplemental Verses
❑ Wonderfully Made: Psalm 139; Hebrews 2:5–9
❑ Deeply Fallen: Geneses 3:1–24; Isaiah 64:6;
Romans 5:12–21; Ephesians 2:1–3

Memory Verse
And we, who with unveiled faces all reflect the Lord's glory, are being transformed into his likeness with ever-increasing glory, which comes from the Lord, who is the Spirit.
2 Corinthians 3:18

Between Studies
Think about people who have been in the news this week. How does the Bible's view of human nature help you to understand them without having to condemn them or put them on a pedestal?

Take time to reflect on all the wonderful ways in which God made you. Thank him for each one. Ask his Spirit to reveal to you those areas where you need his transforming touch.

John 1:1–18
Matthew 27:32–56
Romans 3:21–31

Jesus
Christ

In The Narnia Chronicles, *C. S. Lewis portrays Jesus Christ as a lion named Aslan:*

> "Aslan a man!" said Mr. Beaver sternly. "Certainly not. I tell you he is the King of the wood and the son of the great Emperor-Beyond-the-Sea. Don't you know who is the King of Beasts? Aslan is a lion—the Lion, the great Lion."
>
> "Ooh!" said Susan, "I'd thought he was a man. Is he— quite safe? I shall feel rather nervous about meeting a lion."
>
> "That you will, dearie, and no mistake," said Mrs. Beaver. "If there's anyone who can appear before Aslan without their knees knocking, they're either braver than most or else just silly."
>
> "Then he isn't safe?" said Lucy.
>
> "Safe?" said Mr. Beaver. "Don't you hear what Mrs. Beaver tells you? Who said anything about safe? 'Course he isn't safe. But he's good. He's the King, I tell you."

Christian maturity begins with understanding who Jesus is and what he came to do. Having looked at the greatness of God, the types of revelation, and the two sides of human nature, we are now ready to focus on the person and work of Christ.

His Person

1. Imagine that you are in a group of educated people from a variety of cultural and religious backgrounds. The conversation drifts around to great religious leaders. Among others, Jesus Christ is mentioned. You ask the group if they have any ideas about who he is. "Oh, yes," they reply, and various ones begin to give their opinions. What do you suppose they might say?

2. Read John 1:1–18. Based on this text, what can we know about who the Word is and what the Word did (vv. 1–5, 9)?

3. How is it possible to become a child of God (vv. 10–13)?

How does this miracle take place?

4. When the "Word became flesh" (a human), what did John and others discover about him (vv. 14–18)?

His Work

5. Read Matthew 27:32–56. What specific details add vividness to Matthew's account of the crucifixion (vv. 32–44)?

6. What unusual circumstances immediately follow Jesus' death (vv. 45–56)?

7. What various responses to Jesus are recorded in this passage (vv. 32–56)?

Which response do you identify with most? Why?

8. Read Romans 3:21–31. When you recall Paul's description of humanity in verses 9–20, the situation seems hopeless. Yet what good news does Paul proclaim?

9. Paul uses several word pictures to describe the work of Christ. The word "justified" (vv. 24, 26, 28) is borrowed from the law court. Why has the Judge declared us "righteous" rather than merely "not guilty"?

10. The word "redemption" (v. 24) is taken from the slave market, where a person would redeem a slave by paying money. In what sense were we slaves before coming to Christ (see John 8:31–36; Romans 6:15–23)?

11. The words "sacrifice of atonement" (v. 25) are borrowed from the Old Testament sacrificial system. How has Christ's sacrificial death solved the problems described in verses 9–20?

12. How many times does Paul use the word "faith" or "believe" in verses 21–31?

What does it mean for us to have faith in Jesus Christ?

13. Why is there no other way for us to be reconciled to God apart from Christ's death?

14. God sent his only Son to die a death he did not deserve so that you might have a life you didn't deserve. Spend time in prayer thanking God for his love and for making peace through Christ's blood.

Supplemental Verses

❑ The strength of God's love: Romans 5:6–11
❑ The new covenant: 1 Corinthians 11:23–26
❑ Christ's mission: 1 Timothy 1:15–17
❑ A clean conscience: Hebrews 9:11–15
❑ The blood of Christ: 1 Peter 1:18–19

Memory Verse

Yet to all who received him, to those who believed in his name, he gave the right to become children of God—children born not of natural descent, nor of human decision or a husband's will, but born of God.

John 1:12–13

Between Studies

Read the supplemental verses. Write down any fresh insights you discover about the person and work of Christ.

The apostle Paul explained Christ's death by comparing it to what happens in a law court, a slave market, and a temple sacrifice. What modern analogies might you use to explain Christ's death to a non-Christian? Write these down for future reference.

Acts 2:42–47
Ephesians 1:15–23; 3:14–21

The Church

*If you look in the yellow pages under the listing
"Churches," you might be surprised at what you find. For
example, our phone book includes "Churches—Buddhist,"
"Churches—Scientology," and "Churches—Unitarian Univer-
salist." Just what's going on?*

The term church *is now being applied to any group that
gathers for any religious purpose. But however "church" may
be redefined by contemporary society, we must look to the
Bible for our definition. That is the purpose of this study.*

*We will not attempt to deal with the scriptural technicali-
ties that have sometimes divided Christians over their understanding of the church. The Scriptures do not provide a detailed
blueprint for how the church should be organized. As a result,
churches are as varied as the designs of their buildings.*

*However, behind all the differences within the Christian
church, certain basic issues bind us together. This study will
point to some of these foundational truths.*

---

1. When the word *church* is used, what comes to your mind?

2. Read Acts 2:42–47. Who are the "they" in verse 42?

Even though the word *church* is not used, why would that be a proper inference?

3. What activities do the believers engage in?

4. Which of these activities are vital for the health of the church today, and why?

5. Read Ephesians 1:15–23. What does Paul ask God to do for the church (vv. 17–19)?

6. Although the word "know" is prominent in these verses, how is it different from mere head knowledge?

7. To what does Paul compare the power at work in us (vv. 19–20)?

In what ways do you see that power at work in you and your church?

8. What is the relationship between God, Christ, and the church (vv. 22–23)?

9. How do the words "head" and "body" (vv. 22–23) help you to understand our relationship with Christ?

10. Read Ephesians 3:14–21. What are Paul's primary concerns in this prayer for the church?

11. How are all three persons in the Trinity—Father, Son, and Holy Spirit—involved in answering Paul's prayers?

12. Even though Paul asks for so much, why is he confident that God will answer his prayer (vv. 20–21)?

13. Using Paul's two prayers as your model, pray for your church as a whole and for various members in it—including yourself.

Supplemental Verses
❑ Building the church: Matthew 16:16–18
❑ The church persecuted and scattered: Acts 8:1–8
❑ The body of Christ: Romans 12:4–8
❑ One body, many parts: 1 Corinthians 12:12–13
❑ Christ and the church: Ephesians 5:28–30
❑ The head of the church: Colossians 1:18–24
❑ The heavenly Jerusalem: Hebrews 12:22–24
❑ Living stones: 1 Peter 2:4–10

Memory Verse
Now to him who is able to do immeasurably more than all we ask or imagine, according to his power that is at work within us, to him be glory in the church and in Christ Jesus throughout all generations, for ever and ever!
Ephesians 3:20–21

Between Studies

Based on the passages covered in this study, what elements are essential in defining "church" from a biblical point of view?

In light of the high biblical view of the church, does it surprise you that serious problems can occur within the church? Why or why not?

Recall the various word pictures used to describe the church. In what ways are these helpful in defining the nature and mission of the church?

*1 Corinthians 15:50–58
1 Thessalonians 4:13–5:11
Revelation 20:11–21:8*

Time
and
Eternity

In his book The Weight of Glory, *C. S. Lewis wrote: "There are no ordinary people. You have never talked to a mere mortal. Nations, cultures, arts, civilizations—these are mortal, and their life is to ours as the life of a gnat. But it is immortals whom we joke with, work with, marry, snub, and exploit—immortal horrors or everlasting splendors."*

If men and women in fact have "immortality" written on their souls, then existence does not end with physical death. The Scriptures affirm the reality of both time and eternity. How do these meet in an individual? This study will examine some of the texts that deal with future things.

1. Think of the most recent funeral you attended. In what ways were you forced to face up to your own mortality—and immortality?

2. Read 1 Corinthians 15:50–58. In what sense are we unfit for the kingdom of God (v. 50)?

3. Why is it a mystery that "we will not all sleep" (v. 51) before inheriting the kingdom of God?

4. What is the usual function of a trumpet call?

How does the trumpet call relate to the final defeat of death (v. 52)?

5. How does this ringing victory cry affect your view of death? of the end of time?

6. Read 1 Thessalonians 4:13–5:11. How can ignorance about the Lord's return cause unnecessary grief (vv. 13–18)?

7. What is the difference between healthy grief and grieving "like the rest of men" (v. 13)?

8. According to Paul, what will be the sequence of events at the Lord's return? (Note the trumpet call appears again!)

9. What does this passage say about our ability to predict the date of Christ's return (5:1–2)?

10. What results should the day of Christ's return produce in us (vv. 3–10)?

11. How can we use Paul's words to encourage each other (4:18; 5:11)?

12. Read Revelation 20:11–21:8. Following Satan's doom in verses 7–10, a great white throne is seen (vv. 11–15). Who is seated on it, and for what purpose?

13. On what basis are the dead judged?

What happens to anyone whose name is not in the book of life?

14. How would you describe the Holy City (21:1–8)?

15. Who is granted the right to inherit the Holy City, and who is not?

16. How should the biblical view of the future affect our stewardship of time and energy? our support of world missions? our personal evangelism?

17. Take time now to thank God for the hope we have in Jesus Christ. Ask him for grace to live in a manner consistent with that hope.

Supplemental Verses

❑ Christ's return: Matthew 24:30–31; Luke 17:22–37; John 14:3; Acts 1:11; Hebrews 9:27–28
❑ The Christian's destiny: Matthew 25:31–39; John 11:25–26; Romans 8:22–30; Philippians 1:20–24; Titus 2:11–14; 1 Peter 1:3–5
❑ The non-Christian's destiny: Matthew 25:40–46; Luke 16:19–31; 1 Peter 4:17–18; 2 Peter 2:1–12

Memory Verse

Now the dwelling of God is with men, and he will live with them. They will be his people, and God himself will be with them and be their God. He will wipe every tear from their eyes. There will be no more death or mourning or crying or pain, for the old order of things has passed away.

Revelation 21:3–4

Between Studies

Jesus Christ taught that anyone who spends his or her energy acquiring *things* is a fool (see Luke 12:16–21). Yet the media pushes us to think that possessions bring happiness. How can you keep your possessions from possessing you? How can a clear grasp of time and eternity help you sort out your values and priorities?

Consider how you can spend your time, energy, and resources this week—and all the weeks of your life—in light of eternity.

Leader's Notes

Leading a Bible discussion—especially for the first time—can make you feel both nervous and excited. If you are nervous, realize that you are in good company. Many biblical leaders, such as Moses, Joshua, and the apostle Paul, felt nervous and inadequate to lead others (see, for example, 1 Corinthians 2:3). Yet God's grace was sufficient for them, just as it will be for you.

Some excitement is also natural. Your leadership is a gift to the others in the group. Keep in mind, however, that other group members also share responsibility for the group. Your role is simply to stimulate discussion by asking questions and encouraging people to respond. The suggestions listed below can help you to be an effective leader.

Preparing to Lead

1. Ask God to help you understand and apply the passage to your own life. Unless that happens, you will not be prepared to lead others.

2. Carefully work through each question in the study guide. Meditate and reflect on the passage as you formulate your answers.

3. Familiarize yourself with the leader's notes for the study. These will help you understand the purpose of the study and will provide valuable information about the questions in the study.

4. Pray for the various members of the group. Ask God to use these studies to make you better disciples of Jesus Christ.

5. Before the first meeting, make sure each person has a study guide. Encourage them to prepare beforehand for each study.

Leading the Study

1. Begin the study on time. If people realize that the study begins on schedule, they will work harder to arrive on time.

2. At the beginning of your first time together, explain that these studies are designed to be discussions, not lectures. Encourage everyone to participate, but realize that some may be hesitant to speak during the first few sessions.

3. Read the introductory paragraph at the beginning of the discussion. This will orient the group to the passage being studied.

4. Read the passage aloud. You may choose to do this yourself, or you might ask for volunteers.

5. The questions in the guide are designed to be used just as they are written. If you wish, you may simply read each one aloud to the group. Or you may prefer to express them in your own words. Unnecessary rewording of the questions, however, is not recommended.

6. Don't be afraid of silence. People in the group may need time to think before responding.

7. Avoid answering your own questions. If necessary, rephrase a question until it is clearly understood. Even an eager group will quickly become passive and silent if they think the leader will do most of the talking.

8. Encourage more than one answer to each question. Ask, "What do the rest of you think?" or "Anyone else?" until several people have had a chance to respond.

9. Try to be affirming whenever possible. Let people know you appreciate their insights into the passage.

10. Never reject an answer. If it is clearly wrong, ask, "Which verse led you to that conclusion?" Or let the group

50

handle the problem by asking them what they think about the question.

11. Avoid going off on tangents. If people wander off course, gently bring them back to the passage being considered.

12. Conclude your time together with conversational prayer. Ask God to help you apply those things that you learned in the study.

13. End on time. This will be easier if you control the pace of the discussion by not spending too much time on some questions or too little on others.

Many more suggestions and helps are found in the book *Leading Bible Discussions* (InterVarsity Press). Reading it would be well worth your time.

Study One   The Greatness
                              of God
Isaiah 40:9–31

Purpose: To cast away our puny concepts of God and to rediscover his greatness.

Question 1.
Every study begins with an "approach question," which is discussed *before* reading the passage. An approach question is designed to do three things.

First, it helps to break the ice. Because an approach question doesn't require any knowledge of the passage or any special preparation, it can get people talking and can help them to warm up to each other.

Second, an approach question can motivate people to study the passage at hand. At the beginning of the study, people in the group aren't necessarily ready to jump into the world of the Bible. Their minds may be on other things (their kids, a problem at work, an upcoming meeting) that have nothing to do with the study. An approach question can capture their interest and draw them into the discussion by raising important issues related to the study. The question becomes a bridge between their personal lives and the answers found in Scripture.

Third, a good approach question can reveal where people's thoughts or feelings need to be transformed by Scripture. That is why it is important to ask the approach question *before* reading the passage. The passage might inhibit the spontaneous, honest answers people might have given, because they feel compelled to give biblical answers. The approach question allows them to compare their personal thoughts and feelings with what they later discover in Scripture.

Question 2.

Much of the book of Isaiah is written in Hebrew poetry. One of the most common elements of Hebrew poetry is the use of parallelism, where one statement is similar to or contrasted with a previous statement. Verse 9 opens with "You who bring good tidings," which is repeated a couple of lines later. Yet what follows immediately after the parallel phrase is not straight repetition. Help the group to observe the differences.

Question 3.

Make sure the group digs out everything that's in the text. The list should include qualities of God such as his sovereignty, power, judgment, shepherd-like care, gentleness, creativity, might, wisdom, and understanding.

Question 8.

"Apparently some Israelite doubters were comparing their God with the gods of their captors, and they believed that the Lord was failing the test" (NIV Study Bible [Grand Rapids,

Mich.: Zondervan, 1985], 1073). We may not be so overt with our comparisons, but our loyalties to lesser "gods" indicate that we, too, often put the Lord in second or third place.

Question 12.
The energy discussion is meant to show that every motion can be equally demanding when the time dimension is included. A hundred yard dash may seem to be "high energy" when compared to a walk. But if the walk is for one hundred miles, more energy is required than for the dash.

Supplemental Verses.
Each study includes "Supplemental Verses" that can be read if you would like to see more of what Scripture teaches on the subject. Since these verses are not a part of the main discussion, do not attempt to introduce them in the middle of the study. They are an *extra* resource to be looked up before or after the study.

Study Two   Revelation
Psalm 19

Purpose: To understand how God speaks to us through two types of revelation: his world and his Word.

Question 2.
David starts with general observations about the revelation of God in nature (vv. 1–6) and in the law (vv. 7–10). But in verse 11 and following, the psalm is highly personal: "my hidden faults" (v. 12), "your servant" (v. 13), "not rule over me" (v. 13), "will I be blameless" (v. 13), "words of my mouth" (v. 14), "my Rock and my Redeemer" (v. 14).

Question 3.

"The heavens ceaselessly declare the glory of God; *the firmament,* or extended expanse of the sky, reveals Him by being His workmanship; each day speaks to the following day, and each night makes Him known. While they themselves are silent and inarticulate, their testimony is heard everywhere. *Cf.* Romans 1:19, 20" (*The New Bible Commentary: Revised* [Grand Rapids, Mich.: Eerdmans, 1970], 462).

Questions 5–6.

In question 5, look for such words as "the law of the LORD" (v. 7), "the statutes of the LORD" (v. 7), "the precepts of the LORD" (v. 8), and so on.

In question 6, some of the benefits we receive are "reviving the soul" (v. 7), "making wise the simple" (v. 7), and "giving joy to the heart" (v. 8).

Discovering how the benefits relate to the words the psalmist uses may take some thought. For example, how does the fact that "the precepts of the LORD are right" give "joy to the heart"?

Questions 8–9.

Note that the two kinds of sins listed seem to encompass every sin: (a) "hidden faults" (v. 12), and (b) "willful sins" (v. 13). Theologians refer to these as "sins of omission" and "sins of commission."

Study Three   Human Nature

Genesis 1:24–31
Romans 3:9–20

Purpose: To realize that we are both wonderfully made and deeply fallen.

Question 3.

The words "And God said" start each creative day. God takes the initiative. In the middle of day 6, the wording shifts slightly to "Then God said," suggesting that he is about to do something new when he creates humanity.

The words that normally follow "And God said" are "Let there be." Yet when God begins to create humanity, he says for the first time, "Let us make," a reference to God's own image that will be reflected in the man and woman he creates.

Questions 4–5.

Both the animals and humans are created by God. Yet only the man and woman are created in God's image. Likewise, only they are given the command to rule over the animals and to subdue the earth.

Questions 10–11.

The Genesis text points to human beings as approved by God, in fellowship with him and one another, and views them as "very good." The Romans text points to humans who are disapproved by God, in rebellion against him and at war with one another, and views them as sinful (as does Genesis 3 and following).

Our "depravity" (as theologians refer to it) does not mean that we are as bad as we possibly could be. Rather it means (a) we do not measure up to God's standard of righteousness, and (b) within ourselves we lack the power to change our situation.

A solid biblical view of sin will prevent us from embracing any human as always right and always worthy to be followed. We must never be gullible or naive about humanity's potential for evil.

At the same time, there is always hope for change in those who seem hardened to God and who set themselves against society. Because people are created in God's image and because of the power of the gospel, we must not be cynical or skeptical about the possibility of change.

Study Four   Jesus Christ

John 1:1–18
Matthew 27:32–56
Romans 3:21–31

Purpose: To better understand who Jesus is and what he came to do.

Question 2.

Be sure the eternal nature of the Word is seen. He is united with God, yet he is also separate from God. "Equal but different." Surely we have an indication of God as Trinity here (with the Holy Spirit being mentioned in 1:32). Also note that personality is a characteristic of the Word—he is not a mere force or influence or thought. The Word is a *he*. The Word is, in fact, Jesus Christ. But let this conclusion come from the group as the text is studied. Don't tell. Ask!

Note about "the Word": John wrote at the end of the first century, at a time when Greeks were the leaders in the world of thought and art. Politically the Romans were conquering the world, but Greek was the most common language, and Greek influence was pervasive.

Greek thought made much of the concept of *logos* ("word"), blending ideas of thought and speech into the one word. For years different philosophers, including Plato and Aristotle, struggled with explaining the nature of the universe with concepts about *logos*.

The Jews were also familiar with the Hebrew equivalent of *logos*. After all, it was through God's word ("And God said") that the universe was created.

John, therefore, takes a word familiar to both Greeks and Jews and gives it a startling and fresh definition. For John the Word is not only rational and creative but personal—none other than God himself who became incarnate in Jesus Christ.

Question 3.

We have seen that Jesus Christ is the Word, he is also God, he was present in the beginning with God, he was active in the creation of the world, and he now works with God's power to give those who believe in him the right to become children of God.

We have ignored the paragraph in verses 6–10 which deals with John the Baptist (this is not John the apostle, who wrote this gospel) simply due to time constraints.

Question 5.

As we move to Matthew 27:32–56, Jesus has been arrested, brought before the Jewish leaders on a charge of blasphemy, and found guilty. But the Jews lived under the occupation of Rome and were thus prevented from executing him. So Jesus is dragged to the Roman governor, Pilate, who caves in to crowd pressure (27:20–26) and hands Jesus over to Roman soldiers to crucify him. Our text picks up at this point.

Question 9.

The word *justified* goes beyond mere forgiveness or acquittal. Through Jesus' death and resurrection, our sin and guilt were transferred to him, and his righteousness was given to us. Now God legally declares us as pure and sinless as Christ himself.

Study Five   The Church
Acts 2:42–47
Ephesians 1:15–23; 3:14–21

Purpose: To consider some of the foundational issues that bind us together as a church.

Background.

Confusion exists not only in the yellow pages about how our culture defines the church, but also within the Christian church itself. Just what does "church" mean? The most popular definition is that the church is a building, perhaps with one or more sacred symbols visible outside or inside.

The Scriptures are clear that the church is not a building but the *people of God,* who may or may not make use of a building. In the New Testament, the Greek word translated "church" is *ecclesia,* which simply means "a group of people called out with purpose." This word occurs 115 times. It is translated "assembly" three times in Acts 19, where it refers to a mob that attacked Paul. That's a different kind of assembly!

All other 112 occurrences of *ecclesia* are translated as "church." Twelve out of the 112 clearly refer to the universal church. All other references relate to the local church.

Sometimes the universal church is referred to as the "church invisible," comprised of all those from all ages who have truly believed in the Lord Jesus Christ. This contrasts with the "church visible," who are those living today and belonging to any church, anywhere in the world. Note that membership in the visible church does not assure membership in the invisible church. Although that is the ideal, some people who have never been born from above may attach themselves to the local church.

Question 2.

The context for this group of verses is the dramatic events that took place on Pentecost (see Acts 2:1–41).

Question 3.

"Apostles' teaching. Included all that Jesus himself taught (Mt 28:20), especially the gospel, which was centered in his death, burial and resurrection (see vv. 23–24; 3:15; 4:10; 1 Co 15:1–4). . . . Today it is available in the books of the NT. *the fellowship.* The corporate fellowship of believers in worship. *breaking of bread.* Although this phrase is used of an ordinary meal in v. 46 (see Lk 24:30, 35), the Lord's Supper seems to be indicated here . . . *prayer.* Acts emphasizes the importance

of prayer in the Christian life—private as well as public (1:14; 3:1; 6:4; 10:4, 31; 12:5; 16:13, 16)" (*The NIV Study Bible*, 1648).

Question 6.

"Growth in knowledge is indispensable to growth in holiness. Indeed, knowledge and holiness are even more intimately linked than as means to an end. For the 'knowledge' for which Paul prays is more Hebrew than Greek in concept; it adds the knowledge of experience to the knowledge of understanding. More than this, it emphasizes the *knowledge of him* (verse 17), of God himself personally, as the context within which we *may know what is* . . . (verse 18), that is, may come to know truths about him. There is no higher knowledge than the knowledge of God himself" (John R. W. Stott, *The Message of Ephesians* [Downers Grove, Ill.: InterVarsity Press, 1979], 54).

Question 10.

"I like to think of the apostle's petition as a staircase by which he climbs higher and higher in his aspiration for his readers. His prayer-staircase has four steps, whose key words are 'strength', 'love', 'knowledge' and 'fullness'. More precisely, he prays first that they may be *strengthened* by the indwelling of Christ through his Spirit; secondly that they may be rooted and grounded in *love*; thirdly that they may *know* Christ's love in all its dimensions, although it is beyond knowledge; and fourthly that they may be *filled* right up to the very fullness of God" (Stott, *Ephesians*, 134).

Question 13.

Since the next study will complete this series, you may want to think about what topic you might study after this guide and bring samples to the next session. (Within *The Discipleship Series* you'll find a wide range of topics to pursue.)

Study Six   Time and Eternity

1 Corinthians 15:50–58
1 Thessalonians 4:13–5:11
Revelation 20:11–21:8

Purpose: To consider some of the events surrounding the return of Christ, and how we should live now in light of eternity.

Question 2.

It is often difficult for us to accept the mortality of those we love—especially the members of our own family. Naturally, we do not want them to die, and feel great sadness at the thought of being parted from them. Yet the apostle Paul reminds us in these verses that our current mortal bodies are unfit for the kingdom of God. We, and those we love, *must* be transformed from mortal to immortal, from perishable to imperishable in order to spend eternity together and with God.

Questions 6–7.

Notice that Paul does *not* prohibit us from grieving. Grief over the loss of loved ones is natural, and it seems especially calloused when well-meaning Christians try to bypass the grief process by quoting pious platitudes about heaven.

What Paul forbids is grieving *like the rest of men, who have no hope* (v. 13). Although grief is natural, our grief should be tempered by the fact that death is not the end of human existence. Our loved ones may sleep, but they will one day be awakened by Jesus Christ himself. In the meantime, their spirits are present with him in heaven.

Question 12.

Revelation 20:11–21:8 comes from the closing book of the Bible, and near the very end of it. The Apostle John received a vision while on the island of Patmos (Revelation 1:9), a revelation from the Holy Spirit, dealing with things yet to happen.

The language is colorful, full of imagery, since it deals with issues which none of us has yet lived through.

The poetic and symbolic language of Revelation (which carries a message for all generations) can be confusing if we try to decipher each image and detail. However, the major thrust is very clear: God is preparing his people to live and worship in a new context, apart from sin, because Jesus Christ is worthy to deal with all sin and evil in a final way. Toward the end of this book, Christ treads the winepress of the fury of the wrath of God Almighty (Revelation 19:15). His title is "King of Kings and Lord of Lords." He defeats all enemies in the heavenlies and establishes peace for a thousand years (Revelation 20:1–6).

Question 14.

"The 'Holy City' combines elements of Jerusalem, the temple and the Garden of Eden" (*The NIV Study Bible,* 1949).